CREATE AND Write

More Than 45 Projects for Kids to Create and Write About

Grades 4–6

a television game show

FRACTION ACTION

a label for a can

a menu

ICE CREAM DELIGHTS

a sports shoe

Written by Cyndi Lauritzen • Illustrated by Jon Lyons
Cover Design by Kathy Parks

The Learning Works

The purchase of this book entitles the individual teacher to reproduce copies for use in the classroom.

The reproduction of any part for an entire school or school system or for commercial use is strictly prohibited.

No form of this work may be reproduced or transmitted or recorded without written permission from the publisher.

✻✻✻✻✻✻✻✻✻✻✻ Contents ✻✻✻✻✻✻✻✻✻✻✻✻✻

✻✻✻✻✻✻✻✻✻✻✻✻✻✻✻✻✻✻✻✻✻✻✻✻✻✻✻✻✻✻✻

Introduction

Create and Write is a collection of learning activities uniquely structured to develop in students three recognized components of creativity: flexibility, originality, and elaboration. Each page invites students to create something and then to write about what they have created in any one of three ways. In this manner, **Create and Write** activities encourage creative thinking, individual approaches to specific tasks, and the expression of ideas.

Create and Write activities appeal to students of varying interests and differing abilities. They may be used by individual students, with small groups, or by an entire class. Because each page includes specific instructions to the student, they require little or no teacher intervention and are ideal for enrichment.

Create a Pinball Machine

1. Think of a theme for your pinball machine.
2. Write the theme name at the top of the machine.
3. Decorate your pinball machine, adding color and details.
4. Label each cup with a different point value.

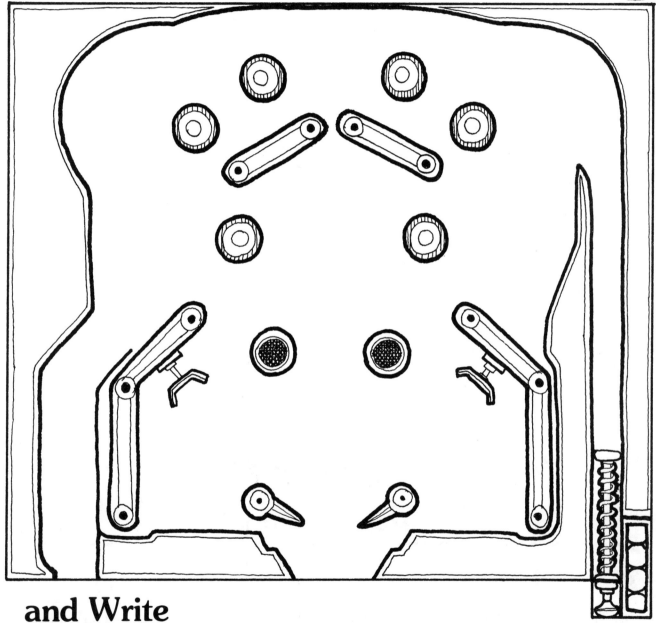

and Write

A. Write a story about "How I Won $5,000 Playing Pinball."

B. The National Pinball Championships are in Chicago this year. Write about your adventures traveling there by train.

C. Make a list of ten different ways you could earn money to help pay for your pinball games.

Create a Cereal

1. Think of a new kind of breakfast cereal.
2. Choose a name for your cereal, and make up a special "box top" offer.
3. Design the package, adding color and details. Include the name and the "box top" offer.

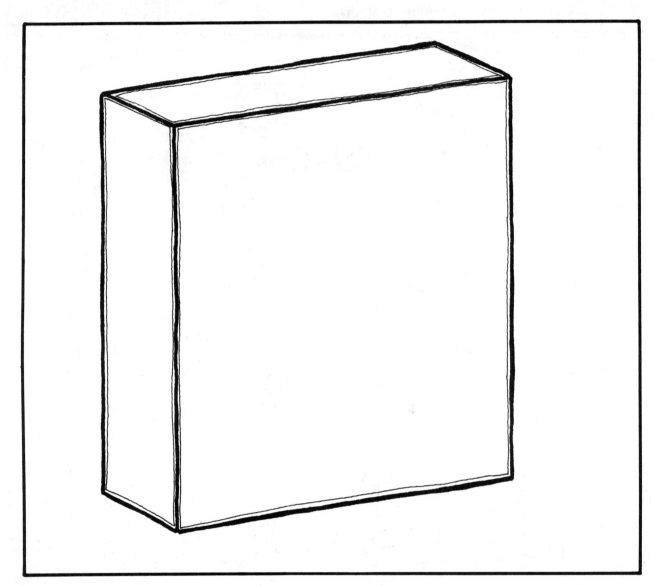

and Write

A. This new cereal has a special magical power. Describe what happens when you eat your cereal and discover this magical power.

B. You've sent in your money for the special "box top" offer, but you haven't received anything. Write an inquiry letter to the company.

C. You are a grocery store manager who ordered 100 boxes of cereal. Tell what happened the day 100,000 boxes arrived because of a computer error.

Create a Secret Clubhouse

1. Cut out the door below.
2. Glue it on a large piece of drawing paper.
3. Draw a clubhouse around the door. Add enough details to show where the clubhouse is located.

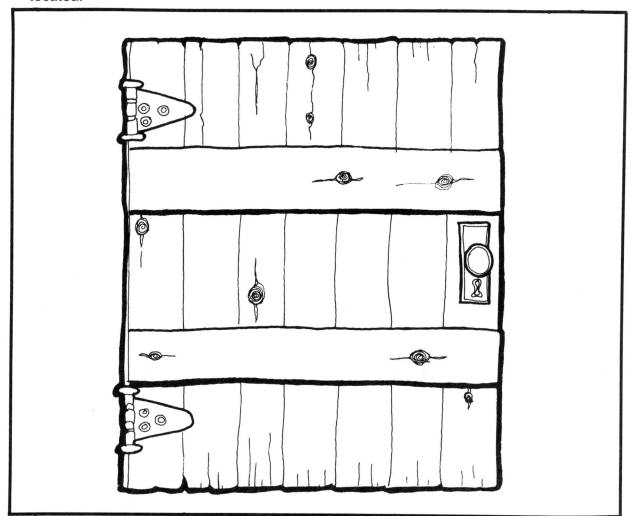

and Write

A. Describe how you would decorate the inside of your clubhouse including furniture, pictures, and special collections.

B. Make up three special code words to use in your clubhouse:
    1. Your secret club name
    2. A password for "Hello"
    3. A password for "Let me in"

C. Write a short story about the clubhouse that begins: "One day when I arrived at the clubhouse, I was surprised to find . . . "

Create an Island Paradise

1. Cut out the shape below and glue it on a piece of paper.
2. Add landmarks and physical features.
3. Make a color key to show several special places on your island paradise.
4. Name your island.

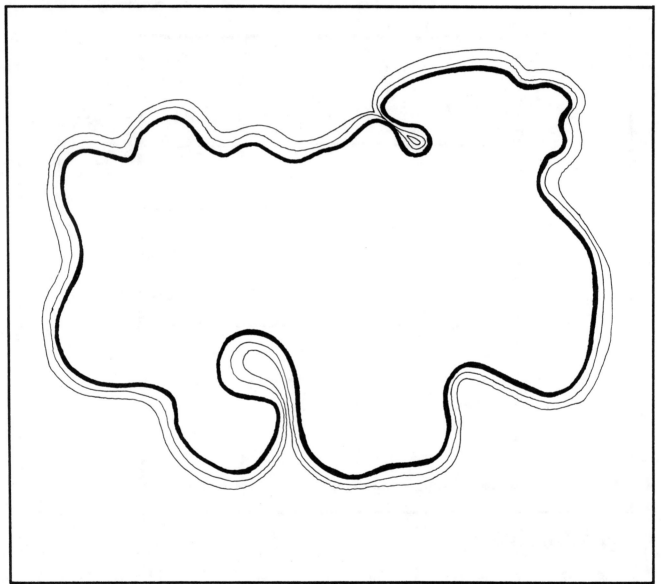

and Write

A. Write about your island paradise. Describe its size, people, climate, language, wildlife, and vegetation.

B. Compare your paradise with where you live. How are they alike? How are they different?

C. Make a brochure for tourists telling about the interesting things to do and see on your island.

Create a Label

1. Think of a fresh fruit drink.
2. Name your drink, and choose a can size and price.
3. Design the label, including all important information such as ingredients, a nutritional value chart, and a logo.

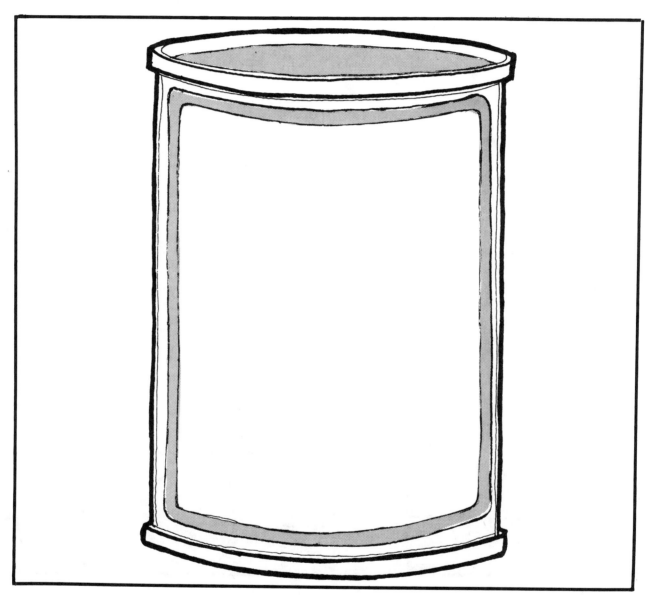

and Write

A. Write a menu for a special family meal that includes this new drink.
B. Write a song about your fruit drink for use in a television commercial.
C. Your soccer team decides to sell this drink to earn money for new uniforms. Write a sales speech you could give to your friends and neighbors to sell your fruit drink.

Create a Toy

1. Cut out the shapes below.
2. Arrange some or all of them to make a toy.
3. Glue your toy on a sheet of construction paper.
4. Add details and color.

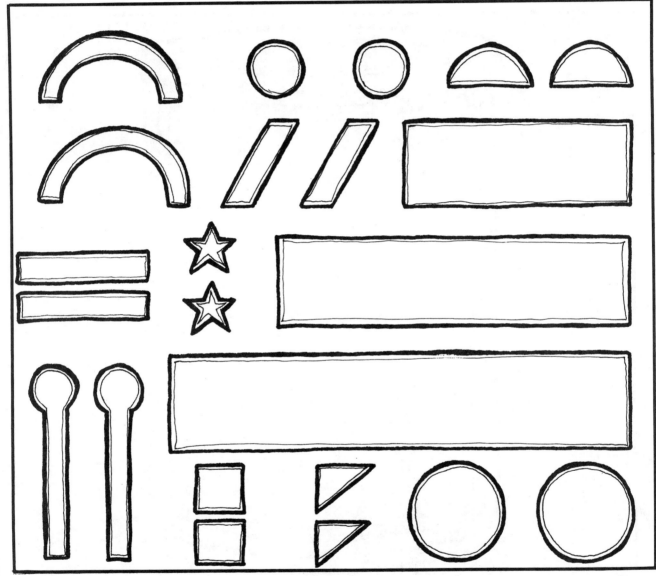

and Write

A. Write an advertisement for your toy as it would appear in a toy catalog.

B. Write a letter to your friends describing how your toy works and why they should get one like it.

C. Design a package for your toy. Be sure to include price, directions for use, age limits, and guarantees.

Create a Sea Monster

1. On a large piece of drawing paper, trace around the sole of your shoe.
2. Turn your shoe outline into a sea monster by adding eyes, a nose, a mouth with teeth, and special features. Color your monster.
3. Color the ocean objects below.
4. Cut out these objects, and add them to your sea monster picture.

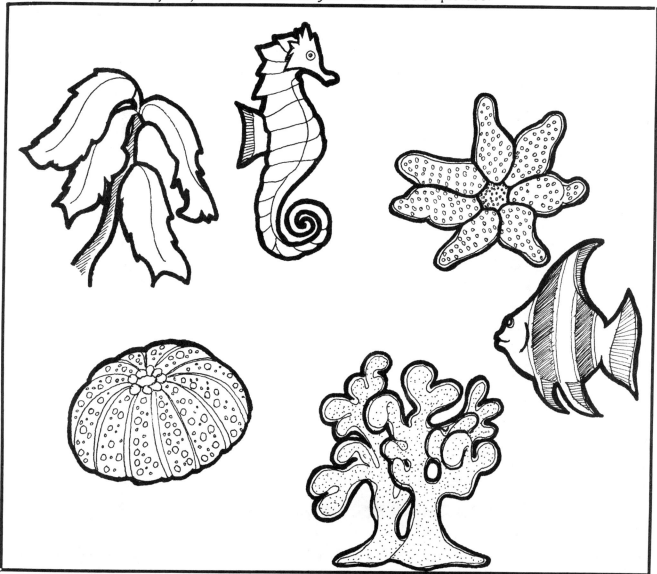

and Write

A. You are an oceanographer who has discovered a monster for the first time. Write a scientific report describing the monster, its habits, and where it lives.

B. Write a short story telling what happens when your sea monster is captured by a newspaper reporter.

C. Describe several ways your sea monster can defend itself against enemies.

Create a Menu Cover

1. Think of your favorite restaurant.
2. Design the menu cover below to advertise the restaurant, adding color and details.

and Write

A. Write a menu listing and describing the food you would like to see served in this restaurant.

B. Write a story entitled "The Mystery of the Missing Menu."

C. You want a job in this restaurant. Write a letter to convince the manager that you should be hired.

Create a Bookmark

1. Cut out the bookmark below.
2. Decorate your bookmark using titles and characters from your favorite books.
3. Punch the hole and add a tassel made of yarn.

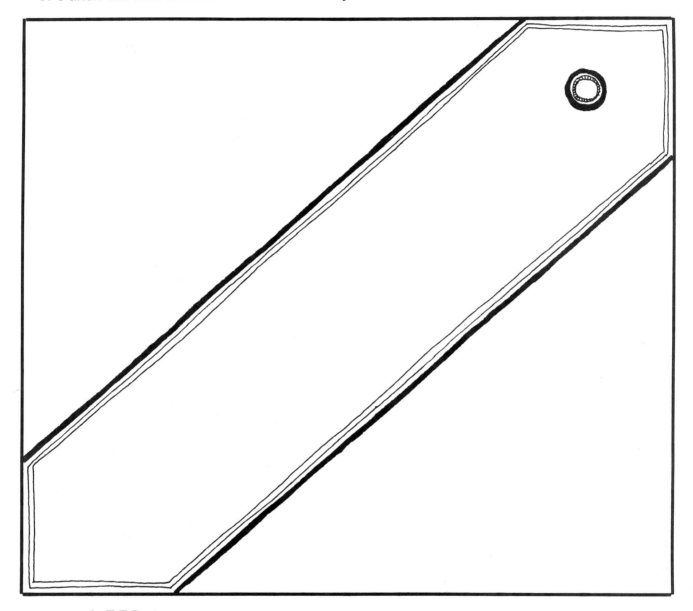

and Write

A. Write an editorial for the school newspaper telling why reading is very important.

B. Suddenly, you **are** the bookmark. Write about the adventure you have when your owner accidentally drops you from a book, and you find yourself lost in an exciting place.

C. You have just finished writing your first book. Write a dedication for the front of the book, thanking the people who helped you.

Create a Super City in A.D. 2000

1. Cut apart the two skylines below.
2. Glue them side by side on a large piece of drawing paper.
3. Add details to make the skyline look like a Super City in A.D. 2000.

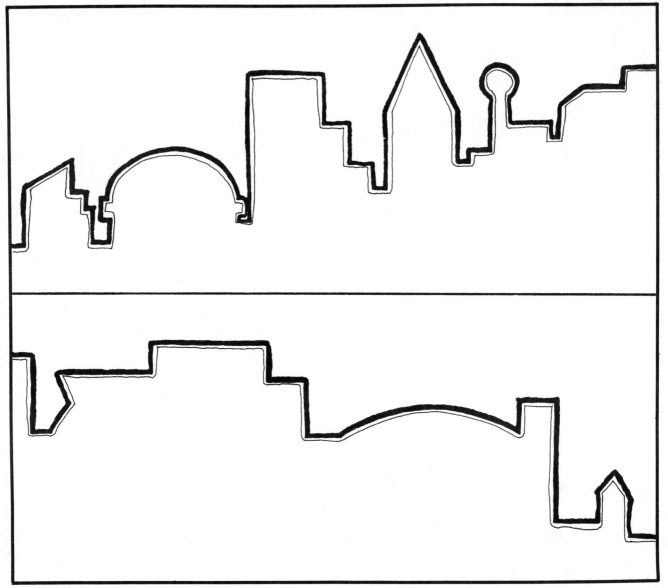

and Write

A. Compare your own city with this Super City. How are they alike? How are they different?

B. List the different kinds of jobs people might have in this Super City.

C. Some of the problems in cities today will be solved by A.D. 2000. Describe the problems you see today and how they have been solved in the Super City.

Create a Seed Packet

1. Think of a new food you would like to grow.
2. Decide on a name, shape, size, flavor, and color for the food.
3. Decorate the seed packet for your new food.

and Write

A. Write the information for the back of the seed packet. Tell how to plant, water, harvest, prepare, and serve the food.

B. Write a creative story about what happens when you plant these seeds but something else grows instead.

C. Your new food product is a success! Overnight you become very wealthy! Write about how your life changes.

Create a Robot

1. Color and cut out the shapes below.
2. Design your robot.
3. Glue the pieces on a sheet of drawing paper.
4. Add details to make your robot special.

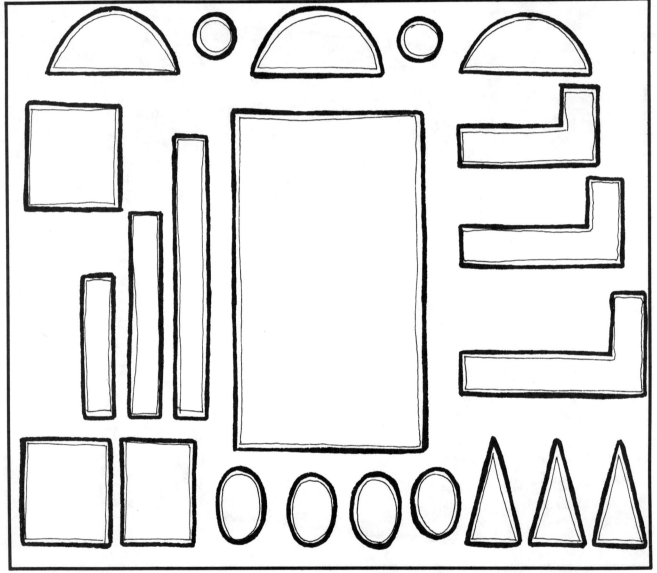

and Write

A. Name your robot and describe three chores it will do for you.

B. Your robot has a mind of its own. It becomes your best friend. Write a story about an adventure you have together.

C. After six months your robot starts making strange noises. Write a letter to the Robot Repair Shop describing the noises and what you think the problem is.

Create a Hot-Air Balloon

1. Cut out the basket below.
2. Glue it on a large piece of paper.
3. Add a hot-air balloon with strings attached to the basket.
4. Decorate the balloon, adding color and details.

and Write

A. Write a farewell speech to your friends before leaving on a two-year trip around the world.

B. Your balloon will take you and your friends to a wonderful secret place for vacation. Write about your adventures at your vacation spot.

C. You are planning a balloon festival for 1,000 hot-air balloons. Write a letter to the local police chief describing how you will handle the traffic, meals, and rooms for everyone coming.

Create a Genie

1. Color and cut out the magic lamp below.
2. Glue it on a large piece of drawing paper.
3. Draw your magic genie coming out of the lamp spout.

and Write

A. Your genie will grant you three wishes. What will your wishes be?

B. Your genie does not speak English! Write a funny story about how you and your genie communicate with sign language and body movements.

C. Your genie is very independent. It refuses to return to the magic lamp. Write about how your life would be different with your genie as your constant companion.

Create a T.V. Game Show

1. Cut out the television below.
2. Glue it on a piece of drawing paper.
3. Add more details to make it look like a real T.V.
4. Draw a picture of your new game show on the screen.

and Write

A. Write some rules telling how your game show works.

B. Write a short story about a contestant who wins many prizes on your T.V. show.

C. If you could visit the filming of any T.V. show, which show would you choose, and what questions would you ask the host?

Create a Mosaic

1. Choose four colors.
2. Use the colors to shade the squares below.
3. Cut apart the squares to make colored chips.
4. Arrange the chips to create a picture.
5. Glue the chips on a piece of drawing paper.

and Write

A. Your mosaic will be displayed on a special wall of the art museum. Write a short speech about the importance of this art form.

B. Write a poem describing your feelings about your mosaic.

C. Your mosaic picture is part of the tile floor in a beautiful castle. Write a story about the castle and the people who live there.

Create a Treasure Map

1. Tear a free-form shape out of the middle of the square below.
2. Glue it on a piece of drawing paper.
3. Color it, and add interesting symbols that can be used as signposts.
4. Mark an X to show where the treasure is buried.
5. Crumple your map to make it look old.

and Write

A. Write directions so that someone else can find the treasure.

B. Write a short story about the adventures of the person who finds your map.

C. Make a list of twenty special objects that you would pack in a treasure box.

Create a T-Shirt

1. Cut out the T-shirt below.
2. Think of a slogan for the front of the T-shirt.
3. Design your shirt using the slogan and two or more colors.

and Write

A. Choose a famous person to receive your T-shirt. Write a letter to the person explaining why you are sending this gift.

B. When you put your T-shirt on , you suddenly find that you become invisible. Write a story about your adventures as an invisible person.

C. Write a funny story about what happens the day your T-shirt is lost at the zoo.

Create a Recipe

1. Think of a recipe for an original main-dish dinner casserole.
2. List the ingredients on the recipe card below.
3. Write the directions for preparing the casserole.
4. Cut out the recipe card.

WHAT'S COOKING? _____

FROM THE KITCHEN OF: _____

SERVES: _____

and Write

A. Your dinner guests are gathering around the table. As you take your casserole from the oven, you realize you've forgotten the main ingredient. What will you do? Write about it.

B. You have entered your casserole in a cooking contest. The judges are tasting it now. Write about what happens.

C. Send your recipe to a leading homemakers' magazine. Write a letter to send with the recipe telling why it should be published.

Create a Money System

1. Think of pictures, slogans, and money values for the new coins and bills.
2. Choose two or more shapes below for your new money.
3. Design the new coins and bills, adding color and details.

and Write

A. Write a funny story about what happens when you try to "spend" your money at the movie theater.

B. Write a letter to the editor of your daily newspaper explaining why your new money system is better than our present one.

C. Write a newspaper story about the good things that have happened in your town as a result of giving away your money to deserving groups.

Create a Kite

1. Cut out the shapes below.
2. Design a kite, adding color and details.
3. Decorate the tail and glue it to the bottom corner of the kite.

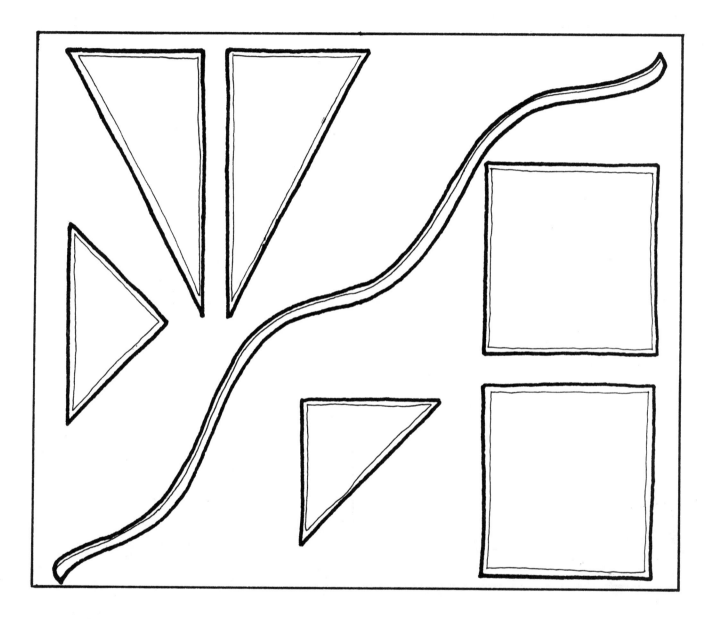

and Write

A. Write a message on your kite that you would like to tell the world.

B. Your kite comes down in the middle of a barnyard. Write a funny story about how you rescue your kite from the animals.

C. Write a poem about the power of the wind.

Create a Storybook

1. Cut out the four pages below on the solid lines.
2. Fold the pages in half on the dotted lines and stack them together.
3. Staple the pages along the folded edge to make a book.

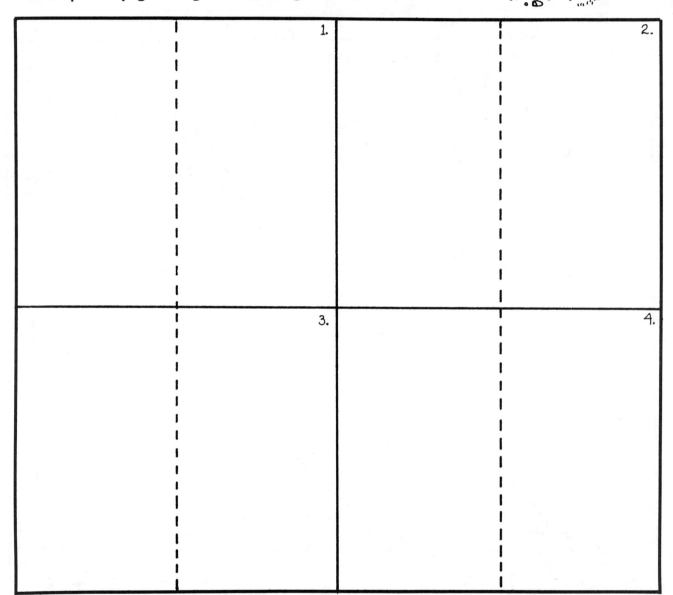

and Write

A. Write and illustrate a fairy tale for your storybook.

B. Write a counting book for a young child to learn numbers.

C. Make your storybook into a joke book with cartoons. Share it with your friends.

Create a Ship in a Bottle

1. Cut out the bottle below.
2. Design a special ship inside the bottle.
3. Add details and color.

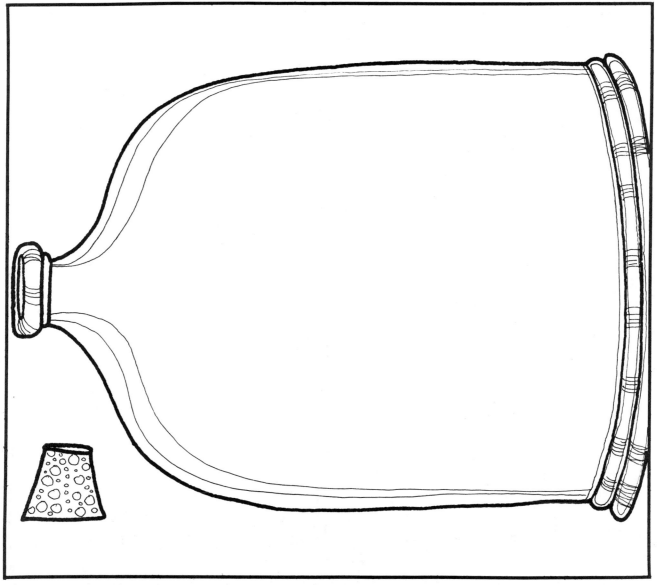

and Write

A. You are shipwrecked on an island. Write about how you survive and how you are rescued.

B. As a royal explorer, write a letter back to the Queen describing your voyage to the New World and the new lands you are claiming.

C. You work on a ship bringing gold from the New World. Write a story about how your ship successfully defends itself against a pirate attack.

Create a Pet

1. Cut out the cage below on the solid lines.
2. Cut slits on the dotted lines.
3. On another piece of paper, draw and color a pet.
4. Cut out your pet and weave it into your cage underneath the slits.

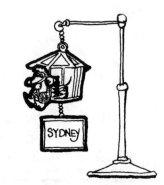

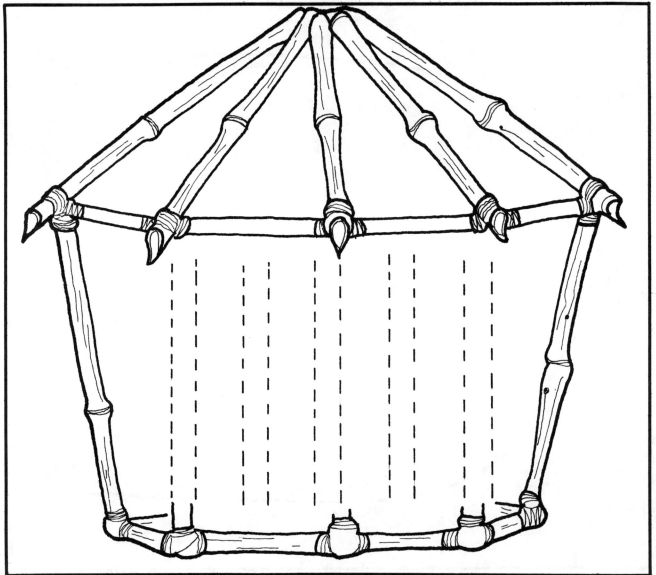

and Write

A. Give your pet a name and write about how you found it.

B. One day you take your pet with you to school. When it's time to go home, the cage is empty! Write about what happens next.

C. You are leaving on vacation, and your best friend is going to take care of your pet. Write directions for its care and feeding.

Create a Postcard

1. Cut out the postcard below.
2. Address the postcard to a close friend or relative.
3. On the front of the postcard, draw and color a picture of your favorite vacation spot.

and Write

A. Write a message to the person to whom you addressed the postcard.

B. Write a short story entitled, "My Life as a Postage Stamp." Tell about your adventures of traveling through the mail.

C. Make a list of all the places in the world you would like to visit.

Create a Machine

1. Cut out the shapes below.
2. Arrange some or all of the shapes to make your machine.
3. Glue them on a piece of drawing paper.
4. Add color and details.

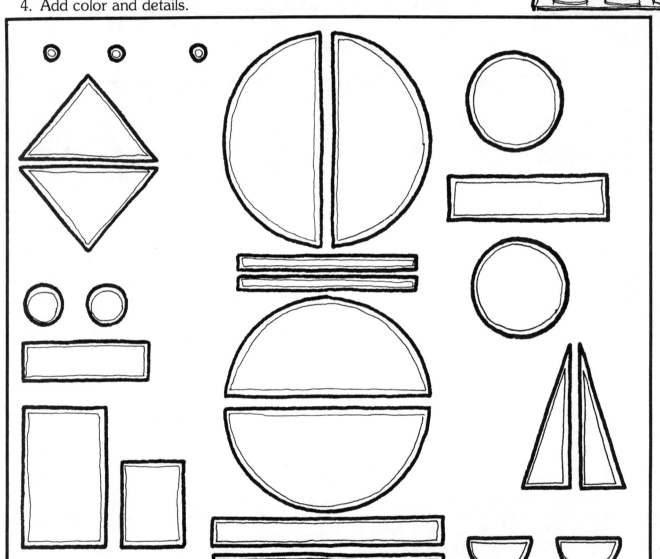

A. Describe what your machine will do that is new and different.

B. Write a magazine advertisement that includes the special features of your machine, the price, and how to order it.

C. Write a business letter to: Design Products, Inc.
   711 Production Way
   Work City, N.Y. 01234

   Ask them to manufacture and sell your machine for you.

Create a Movie Marquee

1. Think of a story line for a new movie. Decide on a name for the movie.
2. Make yourself the star, and choose two Hollywood actors to appear with you.
3. Advertise your movie on the marquee below, adding color and details.

and Write

A. Write an advertisement for your movie to appear in the *T.V. Guide*. Include a short summary of the story line.

B. After opening night, write a critic's review for the next morning's paper. Comment on your acting and on each actor's part.

C. Write a speech for your acceptance of an Academy Award for Best Actor or Best Actress in this movie.

Create a Trophy

1. Cut out the trophy stand below.
2. Glue it on a large piece of drawing paper.
3. Design the top part of the trophy.
4. Fill in the engraved plaque with your name and the achievement for which you won the trophy.

Presented to

and Write

A. Write a letter to your friend telling about how you won this trophy.

B. Write an acceptance speech to give when you receive the trophy at the awards banquet.

C. Write a story about how you can help others to win a trophy by teaching them one of your skills.

Create a Game Board

1. Design, color, and cut out the game board below.
2. Glue the game board on heavy paper.
3. Make cards, game pieces (markers), and a spinner that could be used to play your game.
4. Name your game.

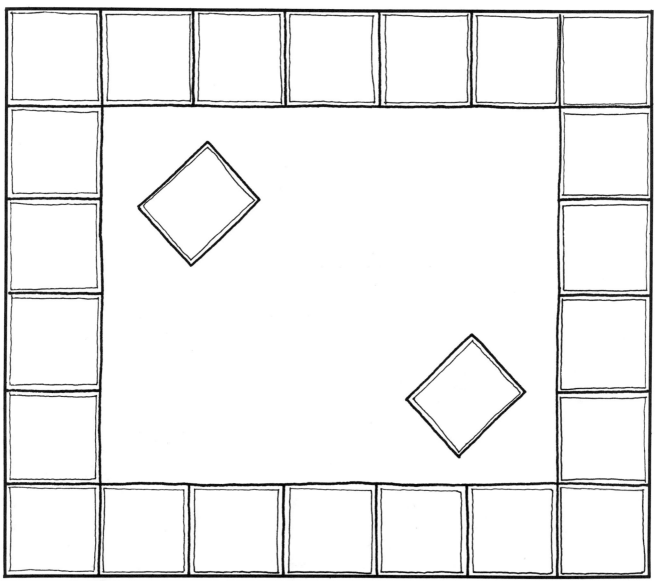

and Write

A. Write directions and rules for playing your game.

B. Write a mysterious invitation to a surprise party where your friends will come to play the new game.

C. Write a plan for a tournament in which ten players will compete for prizes. Describe how you would run the tournament.

Create a Nameplate

1. Color the squares in the grid below so that your name stands out in block letters.
2. Cut around the edge of the grid.
3. Glue it on a piece of drawing paper.
4. Make a border or a frame around the grid and decorate it.

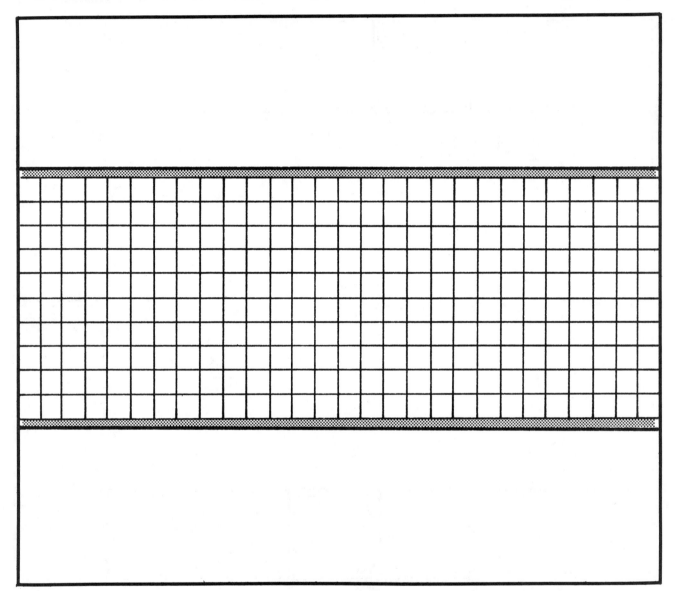

and Write

A. Write a short autobiography. Briefly tell about the important events of your life.

B. Make a list of all the things that make you a special person.

C. If you could be anyone in the world, who would you be and why? Write about it.

Create a Sport Shoe

1. Cut out the shoe below.
2. Add stripes, stars, or special designs to make it a unique sport shoe.

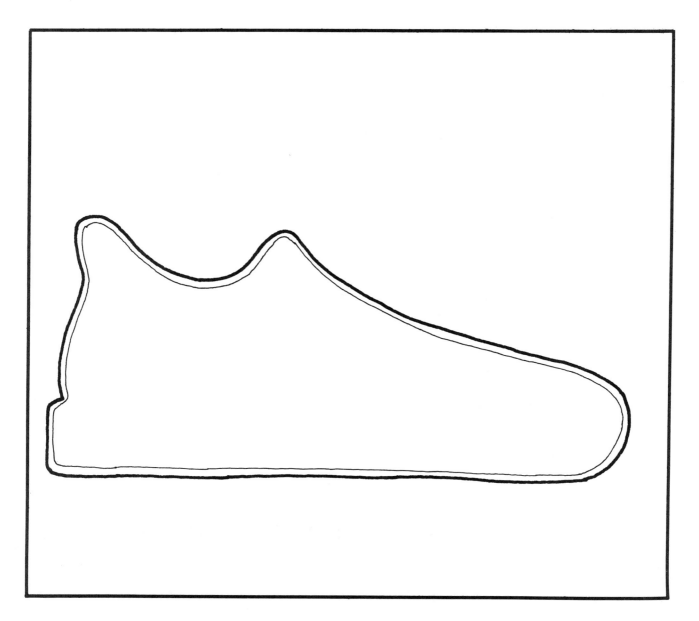

and Write

A. List all the exercises you can think of that will help you stay in shape.

B. Write about a day in your life when you exchange places with your favorite athlete.

C. Make up an exercise and describe how to do it. Write about why your special sport shoe would help athletes do this exercise.

Create an Animal

1. Cut out the shape below.
2. Turn it in any direction, and glue it on a piece of drawing paper.
3. Add color and details to make your animal special.

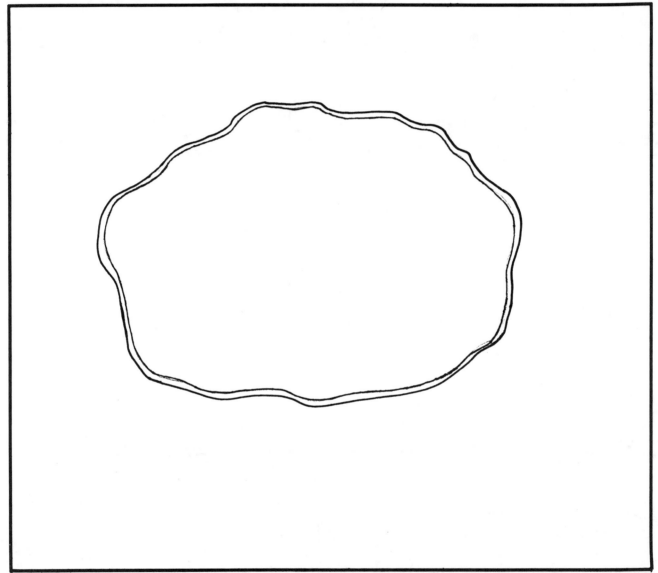

and Write

A. Give your animal a name, and write a short story about it.

B. Describe how the physical features of your animal help it adapt to its environment.

C. Choose another animal. Compare and contrast it to your animal by listing the ways they are alike and the ways they are different.

Create a Spacecraft

1. Cut out the shapes below.
2. Arrange some or all of the shapes to make a spacecraft.
3. Glue the shapes on a piece of drawing paper.
4. Add color and details.

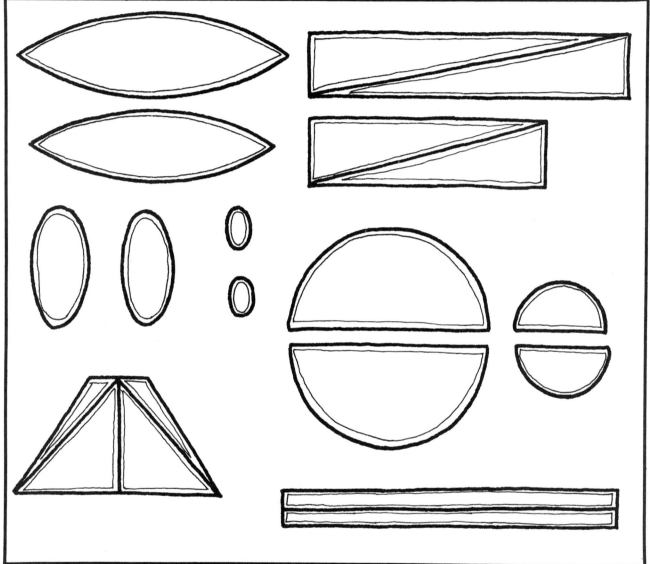

and Write

A. Your spacecraft transports you to a place you have long dreamed of exploring. Write a story about what it's like to be there.

B. Describe the special foods you will need to take on your space trip and how you will prepare and eat them.

C. Write a report about the importance of space travel.

Create a Haunted Castle

1. Cut out the outline of the castle below.
2. Slit the windows on the solid lines and fold them on the dotted lines.
3. Glue the castle on a large piece of drawing paper.
4. Make little ghosts and spooks to paste inside the windows.
5. Add colors and details.

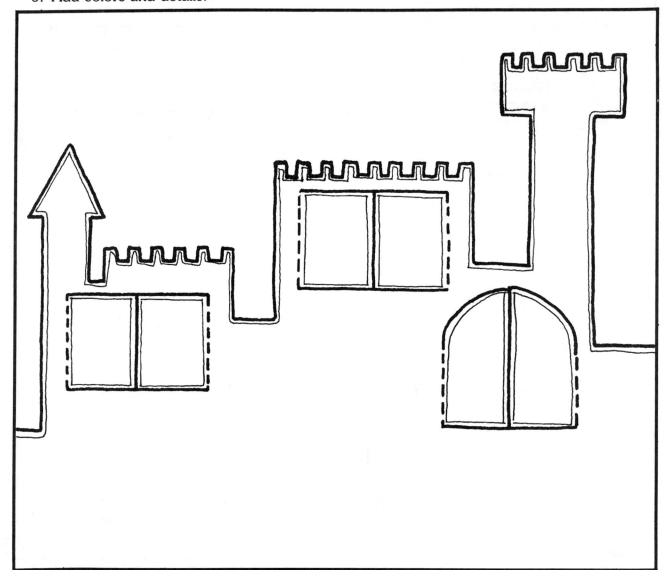

and Write

A. Write a short story about your haunted castle that ends with this line: "I was certainly glad to be home again!"

B. Write about what you did on your favorite Halloween night.

C. You are going to host a Halloween party. Create an original invitation. Also describe the games you will play and the refreshments you will serve.

Create a Health Food Candy Bar

1. Think of a new kind of health food candy bar.
2. Choose a name for your new snack.
3. Design the wrapper, adding color and details.

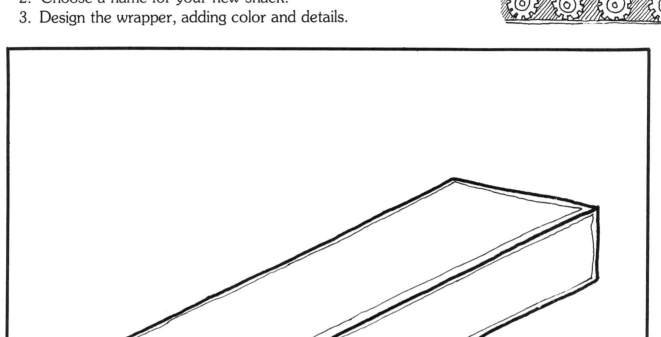

and Write

A. Write a newspaper story about the day you won a year's supply of health food candy bars.
B. Make a list of the wholesome ingredients used to make your new snack.
C. Write about what happened when you traded your health food candy bar for a _____.

Create and Write
© 1982 — The Learning Works, Inc.

Create a Super Sundae

1. Cut out the sundae dish below.
2. Glue it on a piece of drawing paper.
3. Add all the ingredients you need to make a super sundae.

and Write

A. Write a sundae menu describing several gooey delights. One of the choices should be your sundae. Include the prices.

B. Plan a sundae-making contest. Write the rules, including five prize categories.

C. Write a story about what happened the day your refrigerator broke and everything in the freezer melted.

Create a "Critter"

1. Choose two animals from those listed below.
2. On a piece of drawing paper, draw the head of one of your choices with the body of your second choice.
3. Add color and details to make a funny critter.

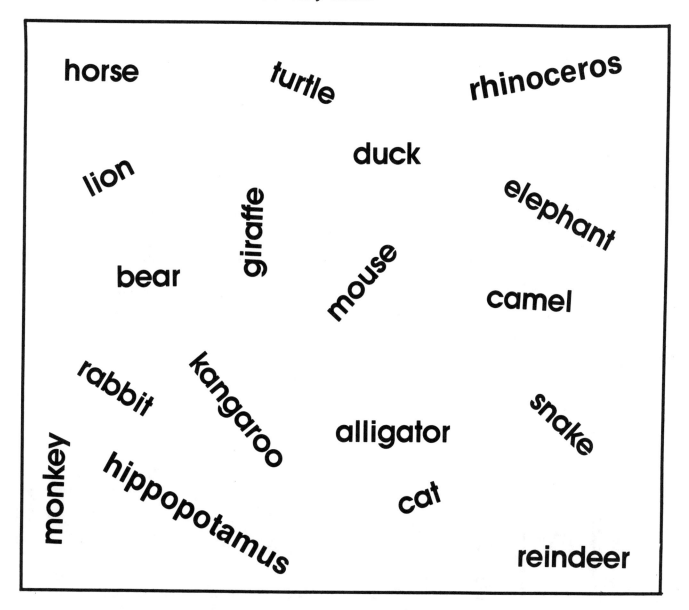

horse   turtle   rhinoceros

duck

lion   giraffe   elephant

bear   mouse   camel

rabbit   kangaroo   alligator   snake

monkey   hippopotamus   cat   reindeer

and Write

A. Write a tall tale featuring your critter as the main character.
B. Write a limerick about your critter.
C. Write an article for a natural history magazine describing the living conditions, social habits, and diet of your critter.

Create a Car of the Future

1. Color the shapes below.
2. Cut them out and design a car of the future.
3. Glue your design on a piece of drawing paper.
4. Add color and details.

LIGHT FRAME   SOLAR COLLECTORS   STRONG, FULL VIEW PLASTIC TOP   NO WEAR RUBBER TIRES

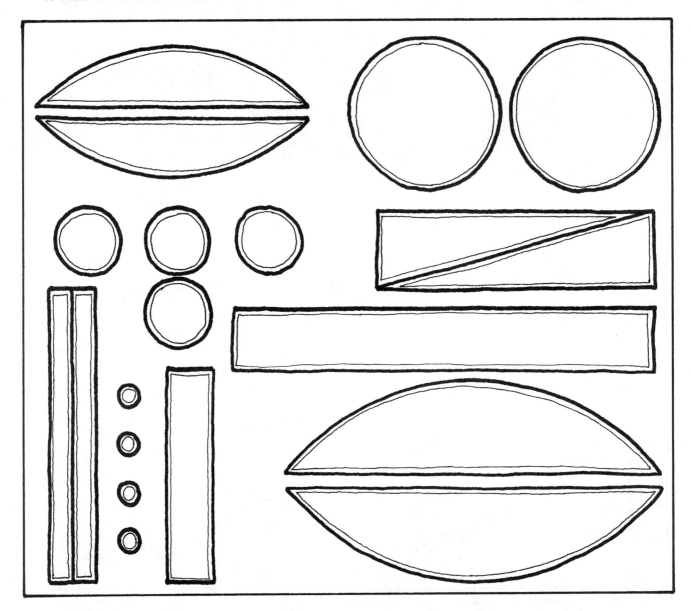

and Write

A. Write a newspaper classified ad to sell your car of the future in today's market.
B. Make a list of all the new and special features of your car.
C. Write a short script for a television commercial to sell your car.

Create a Magic Trick

1. Cut out the magician's hat below.
2. Glue the hat on a piece of drawing paper.
3. Draw something unusual being pulled out of the hat.

and Write

A. Make a list of the different objects magicians use in their magic tricks.

B. Write a short story entitled, "Merlin's Magic Hat."

C. Plan a Music and Magic Show with five acts to entertain your friends and family.

Create a Letter Animal

1. Cut out one of the letters.
2. Glue the letter on a piece of drawing paper.
3. Add lines, color, and details to make a funny animal.

and Write

A. Choose a name for your animal, and write a wonderful fairy tale about it.

B. Write six sentences describing your animal. Use as many words as you can that begin with the animal letter.

C. Describe your animal's two best friends. Tell a story of how they helped each other out of a scary situation.

Create a Badge

1. Cut out the shape below.
2. Design a "Good Going" badge for someone who has done something nice for another person.
3. Give the badge to someone who has earned it.

and Write

A. Write a letter to the person who received the badge, showing appreciation for his or her nice actions.

B. Create a contest so the winners can be awarded your badge. List the contest rules.

C. Write about a time in your life when you deserved to receive a special award.

Create a Billboard

1. Think of a message that reminds people how to help their community, such as "Don't Be a Litterbug," "Save Gas," or "Don't Waste Water."
2. Design a public service billboard that will attract attention, adding color and details to your message.

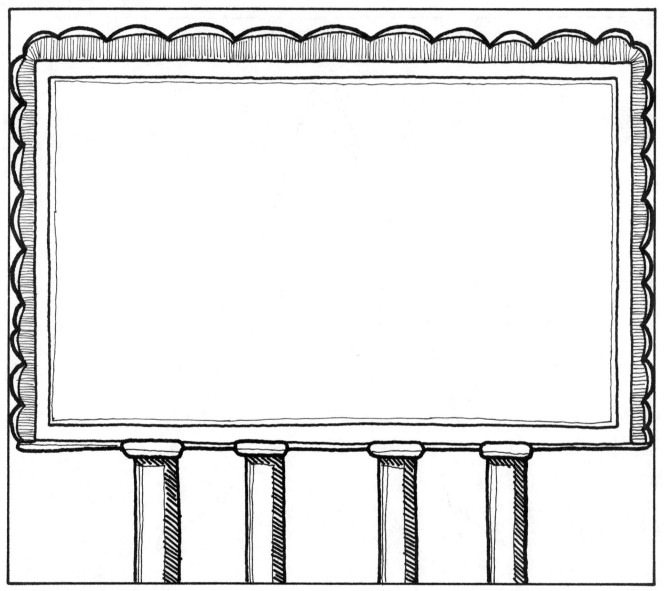

and Write

A. Write a speech to give when your billboard is unveiled to the public.

B. Write a letter to the editor of your daily newspaper telling why billboards like yours should be displayed in other parts of the country.

C. Write a song using the same theme as your billboard to help people remember your message.

Create a Set of Bubble Gum Trading Cards

1. Cut out the four cards below.
2. Decide on a theme for your cards (animals, riddles, sports figures, or famous people).
3. Design and color your four cards. Trade them with your classmates.

and Write

A. On the back of each card, list eight important facts about what is pictured on the front.

B. Make a list of twenty additional cards (five sets of four cards each) that you could include with your trading cards if you were going to sell them.

C. Write a short story entitled "The Secret of Trading Card Success" about someone who has the largest trading card collection in the world.

Create a Cake

1. Think of a special occasion coming up soon for a friend or relative.
2. Design a cake for the special day.

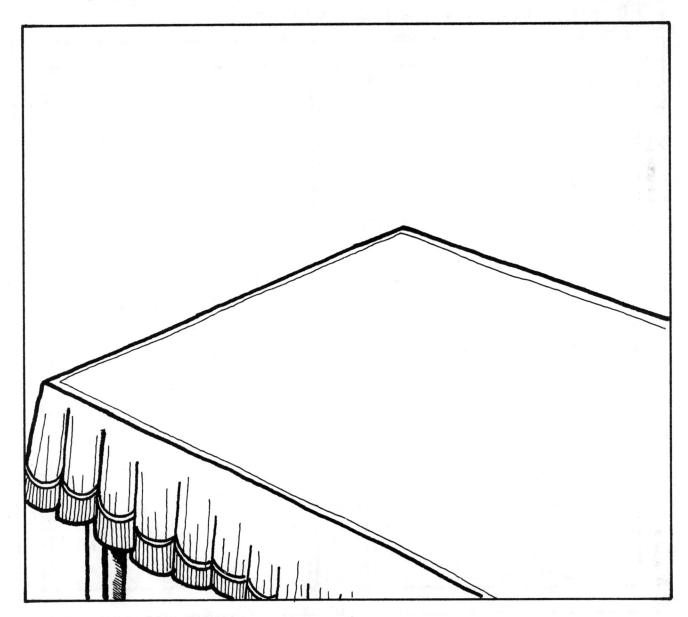

and Write

A. Design an invitation to the party at which you will serve this cake.
B. Write a letter to the bank president explaining why he or she should loan you money to start a new bakery.
C. Write a short story about the day you won the school's annual Cake Decorating Contest.